50 Flavors of the World Recipes

By: Kelly Johnson

Table of Contents

- Mexican Tacos
- Italian Margherita Pizza
- Indian Butter Chicken
- Japanese Sushi
- Greek Moussaka
- Thai Green Curry
- Chinese Dim Sum
- Spanish Paella
- Moroccan Tagine
- French Ratatouille
- Lebanese Hummus
- Turkish Baklava
- Korean Bibimbap
- Vietnamese Pho
- Brazilian Feijoada
- Ethiopian Injera with Doro Wat
- American BBQ Ribs
- Egyptian Koshari
- Jamaican Jerk Chicken
- Argentine Empanadas
- Filipino Adobo
- Cuban Ropa Vieja
- South African Bunny Chow
- Peruvian Ceviche
- Malaysian Satay
- Portuguese Bacalhau
- Russian Borscht
- Swedish Meatballs
- Italian Risotto
- Indonesian Nasi Goreng
- Lebanese Shawarma
- Middle Eastern Falafel
- French Bouillabaisse
- Singapore Chili Crab
- Thai Mango Sticky Rice

- Chinese Kung Pao Chicken
- Indian Samosas
- Italian Lasagna
- Moroccan Couscous
- Filipino Lechon
- Persian Fesenjan
- German Sauerkraut with Sausages
- Greek Souvlaki
- Caribbean Callaloo Soup
- Malaysian Laksa
- Egyptian Molokhia
- Italian Osso Buco
- Turkish Kebab
- Jamaican Patties
- Venezuelan Arepas

Mexican Tacos

Ingredients:

- 1 lb ground beef (or chicken, pork, or vegetarian filling)
- 1 tablespoon olive oil
- 1 onion, chopped
- 2 cloves garlic, minced
- 1 tablespoon chili powder
- 1 teaspoon cumin
- 1/2 teaspoon paprika
- 1/2 teaspoon oregano
- Salt and pepper to taste
- 12 small corn or flour tortillas
- Toppings: shredded lettuce, diced tomatoes, shredded cheese, sour cream, salsa, chopped cilantro, lime wedges

Instructions:

1. In a pan, heat olive oil over medium heat. Add onion and garlic, sauté until softened, about 3-4 minutes.
2. Add ground meat and cook until browned, breaking it up with a spoon as it cooks.
3. Stir in chili powder, cumin, paprika, oregano, salt, and pepper. Cook for another 5 minutes, until fragrant.
4. Warm the tortillas in a dry skillet or microwave.
5. Assemble the tacos by spooning the meat mixture into the tortillas and adding desired toppings.
6. Serve with lime wedges.

Italian Margherita Pizza

Ingredients:

- 1 pizza dough (store-bought or homemade)
- 1/2 cup tomato sauce
- 8 oz fresh mozzarella cheese, sliced
- 1/4 cup fresh basil leaves
- 1 tablespoon olive oil
- Salt and pepper to taste

Instructions:

1. Preheat the oven to 475°F (245°C).
2. Roll out the pizza dough on a floured surface to desired thickness.
3. Place the dough on a baking sheet or pizza stone.
4. Spread a thin layer of tomato sauce over the dough.
5. Arrange slices of mozzarella cheese on top.
6. Bake for 10-12 minutes, until the crust is golden and the cheese is bubbly.
7. Remove from the oven and top with fresh basil leaves, olive oil, and a sprinkle of salt and pepper.
8. Serve immediately.

Indian Butter Chicken

Ingredients:

- 1 lb boneless chicken thighs, cut into bite-sized pieces
- 2 tablespoons ghee (or butter)
- 1 onion, chopped
- 2 cloves garlic, minced
- 1 tablespoon ginger, minced
- 1 tablespoon garam masala
- 1 teaspoon turmeric
- 1 teaspoon cumin
- 1 teaspoon coriander
- 1 teaspoon chili powder
- 1/2 cup tomato puree
- 1/2 cup heavy cream
- Salt to taste
- Fresh cilantro for garnish
- Rice, for serving

Instructions:

1. Heat ghee in a large pan over medium heat. Add onion, garlic, and ginger, sauté until softened.
2. Add the chicken pieces and cook until browned on all sides.
3. Stir in the garam masala, turmeric, cumin, coriander, and chili powder. Cook for 1-2 minutes until fragrant.
4. Add tomato puree and cook for another 5 minutes.
5. Stir in heavy cream, simmer for 10 minutes, until the sauce thickens.
6. Season with salt to taste.
7. Serve with rice and garnish with fresh cilantro.

Japanese Sushi

Ingredients:

- 2 cups sushi rice
- 2 1/2 cups water
- 1/4 cup rice vinegar
- 2 tablespoons sugar
- 1/2 teaspoon salt
- 10 sheets nori (seaweed)
- Fillings: cucumber, avocado, crab meat, tuna, salmon, or shrimp (sliced)
- Soy sauce, wasabi, and pickled ginger for serving

Instructions:

1. Rinse sushi rice in cold water until the water runs clear.
2. In a pot, combine rice and water. Bring to a boil, then reduce heat, cover, and simmer for 15-20 minutes. Let it sit for 10 minutes off the heat.
3. In a small bowl, mix rice vinegar, sugar, and salt. Heat until dissolved, then stir into the cooked rice. Let the rice cool.
4. Lay a sheet of nori on a bamboo sushi mat, shiny side down.
5. Spread a thin layer of rice over the nori, leaving a 1-inch border at the top.
6. Add fillings along the bottom edge of the rice.
7. Roll the sushi tightly from the bottom using the mat. Seal the edge with a little water.
8. Slice into pieces and serve with soy sauce, wasabi, and pickled ginger.

Greek Moussaka

Ingredients:

- 2 eggplants, sliced into rounds
- 1 lb ground lamb or beef
- 1 onion, chopped
- 2 cloves garlic, minced
- 1/2 cup tomato paste
- 1 cup red wine
- 1 teaspoon cinnamon
- 1/2 teaspoon nutmeg
- 1/4 cup parsley, chopped
- 2 cups béchamel sauce (butter, flour, milk, and nutmeg)
- Olive oil
- Salt and pepper

Instructions:

1. Preheat the oven to 375°F (190°C).
2. Slice the eggplants, sprinkle with salt, and let them sit for 15 minutes to remove excess moisture. Pat dry and fry in olive oil until golden.
3. In a pan, sauté onions and garlic, then add the ground meat. Brown the meat, then add tomato paste, wine, cinnamon, nutmeg, salt, and pepper. Simmer for 15-20 minutes.
4. In a baking dish, layer eggplant, followed by the meat mixture. Pour the béchamel sauce on top and spread evenly.
5. Bake for 30-40 minutes, until the top is golden. Let it cool before serving.

Thai Green Curry

Ingredients:

- 1 lb chicken or tofu, cubed
- 1 can coconut milk
- 2 tablespoons green curry paste
- 1 tablespoon fish sauce
- 1 tablespoon brown sugar
- 1 bell pepper, sliced
- 1 zucchini, sliced
- 1 cup bamboo shoots (optional)
- Fresh basil and cilantro for garnish
- Rice for serving

Instructions:

1. In a large pan, heat some oil over medium heat. Add green curry paste and cook for 1-2 minutes.
2. Add chicken (or tofu) and cook until browned.
3. Pour in coconut milk, fish sauce, and brown sugar. Simmer for 15 minutes.
4. Add vegetables and cook until tender.
5. Serve with rice and garnish with fresh basil and cilantro.

Chinese Dim Sum

Ingredients:

- 1 lb ground pork or shrimp
- 1/2 cup chopped green onions
- 1/2 cup chopped water chestnuts (optional)
- 1 tablespoon soy sauce
- 1 tablespoon rice wine
- 1 teaspoon sesame oil
- Dumpling wrappers (store-bought or homemade)
- Soy sauce and chili oil for dipping

Instructions:

1. In a bowl, combine ground pork (or shrimp), green onions, water chestnuts, soy sauce, rice wine, and sesame oil. Mix well.
2. Place a spoonful of filling in the center of each dumpling wrapper. Fold and seal.
3. Steam the dumplings in a bamboo or metal steamer for about 10-12 minutes.
4. Serve with soy sauce and chili oil for dipping.

Spanish Paella

Ingredients:

- 1/4 cup olive oil
- 1 onion, chopped
- 1 bell pepper, chopped
- 1 1/2 cups Arborio rice
- 1/4 teaspoon saffron threads
- 1 cup white wine
- 4 cups chicken or vegetable broth
- 1 lb mixed seafood (shrimp, mussels, squid)
- 1/2 lb chicken, cut into pieces
- 1/2 lb chorizo, sliced
- Peas, for garnish

Instructions:

1. Heat olive oil in a large paella pan. Sauté onions and bell peppers until softened.
2. Stir in the rice, saffron, and wine. Cook for 2 minutes, then add the broth.
3. Arrange the chicken, chorizo, and seafood on top. Cover and simmer for 20-25 minutes.
4. Garnish with peas and serve.

Moroccan Tagine

Ingredients:

- 1 lb chicken or lamb, cut into chunks
- 1 onion, chopped
- 2 cloves garlic, minced
- 1 tablespoon ground cumin
- 1 tablespoon ground coriander
- 1 teaspoon cinnamon
- 1 can diced tomatoes
- 1/2 cup dried apricots, chopped
- 1/4 cup almonds, toasted
- 1/4 cup cilantro, chopped
- Salt and pepper
- Couscous, for serving

Instructions:

1. In a large tagine or pot, heat oil and sauté onion and garlic.
2. Add chicken or lamb and brown on all sides.
3. Stir in spices, tomatoes, apricots, and enough water to cover the meat. Simmer for 30-40 minutes.
4. Garnish with almonds and cilantro. Serve with couscous.

French Ratatouille

Ingredients:

- 1 zucchini, sliced
- 1 eggplant, sliced
- 1 bell pepper, chopped
- 2 tomatoes, chopped
- 1 onion, chopped
- 2 cloves garlic, minced
- 1 tablespoon olive oil
- Fresh thyme and basil
- Salt and pepper

Instructions:

1. In a pan, heat olive oil. Sauté onion and garlic until softened.
2. Add zucchini, eggplant, bell pepper, and tomatoes. Cook until tender, about 10-15 minutes.
3. Season with salt, pepper, thyme, and basil. Serve warm.

Lebanese Hummus

Ingredients:

- 1 can chickpeas, drained
- 1/4 cup tahini
- 2 tablespoons olive oil
- 2 tablespoons lemon juice
- 1 garlic clove, minced
- Salt to taste
- Paprika and olive oil for garnish

Instructions:

1. In a food processor, combine chickpeas, tahini, olive oil, lemon juice, and garlic. Blend until smooth.
2. Season with salt and garnish with paprika and olive oil.
3. Serve with pita bread or vegetables.

Turkish Baklava

Ingredients:

- 1 package phyllo dough
- 2 cups mixed nuts (pistachios, walnuts, almonds), chopped
- 1 1/2 cups unsalted butter, melted
- 2 cups sugar
- 1 cup water
- 1 tablespoon lemon juice
- 1 tablespoon rosewater or orange blossom water (optional)

Instructions:

1. Preheat oven to 350°F (175°C).
2. Brush a 9x13-inch baking dish with melted butter. Layer 8 sheets of phyllo dough, brushing each sheet with butter.
3. Sprinkle a thin layer of chopped nuts on top.
4. Repeat the process, layering 8 more sheets of phyllo dough, buttering each sheet, and adding another layer of nuts. Continue until all dough and nuts are used, finishing with 8 layers of phyllo dough on top.
5. Using a sharp knife, cut the baklava into squares or diamonds.
6. Bake for 40-45 minutes until golden and crispy.
7. While baklava bakes, make the syrup: Combine sugar, water, and lemon juice in a saucepan. Bring to a boil, then simmer for 10 minutes. Add rosewater, if using.
8. Once baklava is done, pour hot syrup over it. Let it soak for several hours or overnight before serving.

Korean Bibimbap

Ingredients:

- 2 cups cooked rice (preferably short-grain)
- 1/2 lb ground beef or chicken (optional)
- 1/2 zucchini, julienned
- 1/2 carrot, julienned
- 1 cup spinach
- 2 eggs
- 2 tablespoons sesame oil
- 2 tablespoons soy sauce
- 1 tablespoon gochujang (Korean chili paste)
- 1 tablespoon rice vinegar
- 1 teaspoon sugar
- Sesame seeds for garnish
- 1 tablespoon vegetable oil
- Pickled radish (optional)

Instructions:

1. Cook rice and set aside.
2. Sauté ground beef or chicken in sesame oil and soy sauce, set aside.
3. In the same pan, cook zucchini and carrots separately until tender. Sauté spinach in sesame oil for 2-3 minutes.
4. Fry eggs sunny-side up.
5. In a bowl, combine gochujang, rice vinegar, and sugar to make the sauce.
6. Assemble the bibimbap by placing rice at the bottom of a bowl. Top with vegetables, cooked meat, fried egg, and a drizzle of sauce.
7. Garnish with sesame seeds and serve with pickled radish if desired.

Vietnamese Pho

Ingredients:

- 1 lb beef bones (or chicken for chicken pho)
- 1 onion, halved
- 1 ginger root, halved
- 3-4 star anise
- 2-3 cloves
- 1 cinnamon stick
- 2-3 tablespoons fish sauce
- 1 tablespoon sugar
- 8 cups water
- 1 lb rice noodles (pho noodles)
- 1/2 lb thinly sliced beef (sirloin, flank steak, or brisket)
- Fresh herbs: cilantro, Thai basil, and mint
- Bean sprouts, lime wedges, and chili peppers for garnish

Instructions:

1. Char onion and ginger over an open flame or in a dry pan until browned.
2. In a large pot, combine bones, onion, ginger, star anise, cloves, cinnamon, fish sauce, and sugar. Add water and bring to a boil. Lower heat and simmer for 3-4 hours.
3. Strain the broth, discarding solids. Taste and adjust seasoning with more fish sauce or sugar if needed.
4. Cook rice noodles according to package instructions and divide into bowls.
5. Pour hot broth over the noodles and top with thinly sliced beef (it will cook in the hot broth).
6. Garnish with fresh herbs, bean sprouts, lime wedges, and chili peppers.

Brazilian Feijoada

Ingredients:

- 1 lb black beans, soaked overnight
- 1 lb pork shoulder, cut into chunks
- 1/2 lb chorizo, sliced
- 1/2 lb smoked sausage, sliced
- 1/2 lb bacon, diced
- 1 onion, chopped
- 4 cloves garlic, minced
- 2 bay leaves
- 1 teaspoon cumin
- Salt and pepper to taste
- 1/4 cup chopped cilantro
- Cooked rice for serving
- Orange slices for garnish

Instructions:

1. In a large pot, cook bacon until crispy. Add pork shoulder, sausages, onion, and garlic, and cook until browned.
2. Add black beans, bay leaves, cumin, salt, and pepper, and cover with water.
3. Bring to a boil, then reduce heat and simmer for 2-3 hours, or until the beans and meats are tender.
4. Adjust seasoning and stir in cilantro.
5. Serve with rice and garnish with orange slices.

Ethiopian Injera with Doro Wat

Injera Ingredients:

- 2 cups teff flour
- 1/2 cup all-purpose flour
- 1 1/2 cups water
- 1/4 teaspoon salt

Doro Wat Ingredients:

- 2 lbs chicken drumsticks or thighs
- 2 onions, chopped
- 4 cloves garlic, minced
- 1 tablespoon ginger, minced
- 2 tablespoons berbere spice mix
- 1 can diced tomatoes
- 1/2 cup chicken broth
- 4 boiled eggs
- 1/4 cup niter kibbeh (spiced clarified butter)
- Salt and pepper to taste

Instructions:

For Injera:

1. Mix teff flour, all-purpose flour, and water in a bowl. Let sit for 1-2 days to ferment.
2. Heat a large skillet over medium heat and pour a thin layer of batter to form a pancake-like circle. Cook until bubbles form, then cover and steam for 2-3 minutes.

For Doro Wat:

1. Sauté onions, garlic, and ginger in niter kibbeh until soft and aromatic.
2. Add berbere spice mix and cook for 1-2 minutes.
3. Add chicken, tomatoes, and chicken broth. Simmer for 30-40 minutes until chicken is tender.
4. Add boiled eggs, cooking for an additional 10 minutes.
5. Serve with injera.

American BBQ Ribs

Ingredients:

- 2 racks baby back ribs
- 1/4 cup brown sugar
- 2 tablespoons paprika
- 1 tablespoon chili powder
- 1 tablespoon garlic powder
- 1 teaspoon onion powder
- 1 teaspoon cumin
- Salt and pepper to taste
- 2 cups BBQ sauce

Instructions:

1. Preheat oven to 275°F (135°C). Remove the silver skin from the ribs.
2. Mix brown sugar, paprika, chili powder, garlic powder, onion powder, cumin, salt, and pepper.
3. Rub the spice mixture evenly over the ribs.
4. Wrap ribs in foil and bake for 2.5-3 hours.
5. Preheat grill to medium heat. Unwrap ribs, brush with BBQ sauce, and grill for 5-10 minutes, basting with sauce.
6. Serve with more BBQ sauce.

Egyptian Koshari

Ingredients:

- 1 cup lentils
- 1 cup rice
- 1 cup macaroni
- 1 onion, sliced
- 2 cloves garlic, minced
- 2 cups tomato sauce
- 1 teaspoon cumin
- 1/4 teaspoon cinnamon
- Salt and pepper to taste
- Fried onions for garnish
- Hot sauce for serving

Instructions:

1. Cook lentils, rice, and macaroni separately.
2. Sauté onions and garlic until caramelized, then stir in tomato sauce, cumin, cinnamon, salt, and pepper. Simmer for 15 minutes.
3. Layer rice, lentils, and macaroni on a plate. Pour tomato sauce mixture on top.
4. Garnish with fried onions and serve with hot sauce.

Jamaican Jerk Chicken

Ingredients:

- 4 chicken thighs or breasts
- 2 tablespoons allspice
- 1 teaspoon thyme
- 1/2 teaspoon cinnamon
- 1/2 teaspoon nutmeg
- 1 scotch bonnet pepper (or jalapeño)
- 1 onion, chopped
- 2 cloves garlic, minced
- 1/4 cup soy sauce
- 2 tablespoons brown sugar
- 2 tablespoons lime juice
- Salt and pepper to taste

Instructions:

1. Blend allspice, thyme, cinnamon, nutmeg, scotch bonnet, onion, garlic, soy sauce, brown sugar, and lime juice to make a marinade.
2. Coat chicken in the marinade and refrigerate for at least 2 hours (overnight is better).
3. Grill or bake the chicken at 375°F (190°C) for 30-40 minutes until fully cooked.
4. Serve with rice and beans.

Argentine Empanadas

Ingredients:

- 1 lb ground beef
- 1 onion, chopped
- 1 hard-boiled egg, chopped
- 1/4 cup green olives, chopped
- 1/4 cup raisins (optional)
- 1 tablespoon paprika
- Salt and pepper to taste
- Empanada dough discs (store-bought or homemade)
- Olive oil for frying

Instructions:

1. In a pan, sauté onions until softened, then add ground beef and cook until browned.
2. Stir in paprika, salt, pepper, olives, raisins, and hard-boiled egg.
3. Place a spoonful of filling on each empanada dough disc, fold over, and crimp the edges to seal.
4. Fry empanadas in hot oil until golden and crispy, about 3-4 minutes.
5. Serve hot.

Filipino Adobo

Ingredients:

- 2 lbs chicken or pork (or a mix of both)
- 1/2 cup soy sauce
- 1/4 cup vinegar
- 1 onion, sliced
- 4 cloves garlic, minced
- 2 bay leaves
- 1 teaspoon black peppercorns
- 1/2 teaspoon sugar
- 1/2 cup water
- Salt to taste
- Cooked rice for serving

Instructions:

1. In a large bowl, combine soy sauce, vinegar, garlic, onion, bay leaves, peppercorns, and sugar. Add the chicken or pork and marinate for at least 30 minutes.
2. In a large pot, heat the marinated meat along with the marinade. Add water and bring to a boil.
3. Reduce the heat and simmer for 40-45 minutes, or until the meat is tender and the sauce thickens slightly.
4. Adjust seasoning with salt and serve with rice.

Cuban Ropa Vieja

Ingredients:

- 2 lbs flank steak or skirt steak
- 1 onion, sliced
- 1 bell pepper, sliced
- 4 cloves garlic, minced
- 2 cups tomato sauce
- 1/2 cup dry white wine
- 1 teaspoon cumin
- 1 teaspoon oregano
- 1/2 teaspoon paprika
- 1 bay leaf
- Salt and pepper to taste
- Fresh cilantro for garnish
- Cooked rice for serving

Instructions:

1. In a large pot, cook the beef in water for about 2 hours, or until tender. Remove the beef and shred it with forks.
2. In the same pot, sauté the onion, bell pepper, and garlic until softened.
3. Add tomato sauce, wine, cumin, oregano, paprika, and bay leaf. Simmer for 10-15 minutes.
4. Add shredded beef and cook for an additional 20 minutes, stirring occasionally.
5. Season with salt and pepper, then garnish with fresh cilantro and serve with rice.

South African Bunny Chow

Ingredients:

- 2 cups cooked lamb or chicken (or vegetarian)
- 2 tablespoons vegetable oil
- 1 onion, chopped
- 2 cloves garlic, minced
- 1 tablespoon curry powder
- 1 teaspoon turmeric
- 1 teaspoon cumin
- 2 tomatoes, chopped
- 1/2 cup water
- Salt and pepper to taste
- 2 loaves white bread (hollowed out)
- Fresh cilantro for garnish

Instructions:

1. In a large pan, heat the vegetable oil and sauté onions and garlic until softened.
2. Add curry powder, turmeric, and cumin, and cook for another minute.
3. Stir in chopped tomatoes and cook until they break down, forming a sauce.
4. Add the cooked lamb or chicken and water. Simmer for 20-25 minutes.
5. Season with salt and pepper.
6. Hollow out the bread loaves, creating small bowls. Fill each with the curry mixture and garnish with fresh cilantro.

Peruvian Ceviche

Ingredients:

- 1 lb fresh white fish (such as tilapia or snapper), cut into small cubes
- 1 red onion, thinly sliced
- 2-3 limes, juiced
- 1 lemon, juiced
- 2-3 small hot chilies (like jalapeños), sliced
- 1 tablespoon fresh cilantro, chopped
- Salt and pepper to taste
- Sweet potato and corn for serving (optional)

Instructions:

1. In a large bowl, combine the fish, lime juice, lemon juice, and chilies. Stir gently to coat the fish in the citrus juices.
2. Let it marinate for 15-20 minutes, or until the fish becomes opaque and "cooked."
3. Add the red onion and cilantro, then season with salt and pepper.
4. Serve with boiled sweet potato and corn on the side, if desired.

Malaysian Satay

Ingredients:

- 1 lb chicken or beef, cut into small cubes
- 1/4 cup soy sauce
- 1 tablespoon brown sugar
- 2 cloves garlic, minced
- 1 tablespoon ginger, minced
- 1 tablespoon curry powder
- 1/2 teaspoon turmeric
- 1 tablespoon peanut butter
- Skewers (wooden or metal)

Instructions:

1. In a bowl, combine soy sauce, brown sugar, garlic, ginger, curry powder, turmeric, and peanut butter.
2. Add the chicken or beef cubes and marinate for at least 1 hour.
3. Thread the meat onto skewers.
4. Grill or pan-fry the skewers for 3-5 minutes per side, or until cooked through.
5. Serve with a peanut dipping sauce.

Portuguese Bacalhau

Ingredients:

- 1 lb salted cod (bacalhau), soaked overnight and desalted
- 4 medium potatoes, sliced
- 1 onion, sliced
- 4 cloves garlic, minced
- 1/4 cup olive oil
- 1/4 cup fresh parsley, chopped
- Salt and pepper to taste

Instructions:

1. Preheat the oven to 375°F (190°C).
2. In a large skillet, sauté onions and garlic in olive oil until softened.
3. Layer the bottom of a baking dish with sliced potatoes. Top with a layer of desalted cod, then onions and garlic mixture. Drizzle with more olive oil.
4. Bake for 30-35 minutes, until the potatoes are tender.
5. Garnish with parsley and serve.

Russian Borscht

Ingredients:

- 2 medium beets, peeled and grated
- 1 onion, chopped
- 2 carrots, chopped
- 1 potato, diced
- 1/2 head of cabbage, shredded
- 1 tablespoon tomato paste
- 4 cups beef broth (or vegetable broth)
- 2 tablespoons vinegar
- 1 tablespoon sugar
- Salt and pepper to taste
- Sour cream for serving
- Fresh dill for garnish

Instructions:

1. In a large pot, sauté onions, carrots, and beets in a bit of oil for about 5 minutes.
2. Add potato, cabbage, tomato paste, and broth. Bring to a boil.
3. Reduce heat and simmer for 30-40 minutes, until the vegetables are tender.
4. Stir in vinegar, sugar, salt, and pepper to taste.
5. Serve with a dollop of sour cream and garnish with fresh dill.

Swedish Meatballs

Ingredients:

- 1 lb ground beef
- 1/2 lb ground pork
- 1/2 onion, finely chopped
- 1/4 cup breadcrumbs
- 1/4 cup milk
- 1 egg
- Salt and pepper to taste
- 2 tablespoons butter
- 1/4 cup flour
- 2 cups beef broth
- 1/4 cup heavy cream
- 1 tablespoon soy sauce

Instructions:

1. In a bowl, combine ground beef, ground pork, onion, breadcrumbs, milk, egg, salt, and pepper. Shape into small meatballs.
2. In a skillet, heat butter and brown the meatballs in batches.
3. Remove meatballs and set aside. In the same skillet, add flour and cook for 2 minutes.
4. Gradually whisk in beef broth, heavy cream, and soy sauce. Simmer until thickened.
5. Return meatballs to the sauce and cook for an additional 10-15 minutes.
6. Serve with mashed potatoes or lingonberry sauce.

Italian Risotto

Ingredients:

- 1 cup Arborio rice
- 4 cups chicken or vegetable broth
- 1/2 cup dry white wine
- 1 onion, chopped
- 2 cloves garlic, minced
- 2 tablespoons butter
- 1/4 cup grated Parmesan cheese
- Salt and pepper to taste
- Fresh parsley for garnish

Instructions:

1. In a large pot, heat the broth and keep it warm.
2. In a separate pan, sauté onions and garlic in butter until softened.
3. Add rice and cook for 1-2 minutes, stirring to coat the rice in butter.
4. Pour in white wine and cook until absorbed.
5. Gradually add the warm broth, one ladle at a time, stirring constantly until absorbed before adding more.
6. Once the rice is tender and creamy, stir in Parmesan cheese, salt, and pepper.
7. Serve with fresh parsley.

Indonesian Nasi Goreng

Ingredients:

- 3 cups cooked rice (preferably day-old)
- 2 tablespoons vegetable oil
- 2 cloves garlic, minced
- 1 onion, chopped
- 1 red bell pepper, chopped
- 1/2 cup cooked chicken or shrimp (optional)
- 2 eggs, scrambled
- 2 tablespoons soy sauce
- 1 tablespoon kecap manis (sweet soy sauce)
- 1 tablespoon sambal oelek (chili paste)
- Fresh cucumber and tomato for garnish

Instructions:

1. Heat oil in a large pan and sauté garlic, onion, and bell pepper until softened.
2. Add cooked rice, chicken or shrimp (if using), and scrambled eggs. Stir-fry for a few minutes.
3. Add soy sauce, kecap manis, and sambal oelek. Stir well to coat the rice.
4. Serve with cucumber and tomato on the side.

Lebanese Shawarma

Ingredients:

- 2 lbs chicken thighs, boneless and skinless
- 1 tablespoon cumin
- 1 tablespoon paprika
- 1 tablespoon garlic powder
- 1 teaspoon turmeric
- 1 teaspoon cinnamon
- 1 tablespoon olive oil
- 1/4 cup lemon juice
- 1/4 cup yogurt
- Salt and pepper to taste
- Pita bread, for serving
- Hummus, garlic sauce, and pickles for garnish

Instructions:

1. In a bowl, combine cumin, paprika, garlic powder, turmeric, cinnamon, olive oil, lemon juice, yogurt, salt, and pepper. Coat chicken in the marinade and refrigerate for at least 2 hours.
2. Grill or pan-cook the chicken until cooked through, then slice into thin strips.
3. Serve on pita bread with hummus, garlic sauce, and pickles.

Middle Eastern Falafel

Ingredients:

- 2 cups dried chickpeas (soaked overnight)
- 1 onion, chopped
- 4 cloves garlic, minced
- 1/4 cup fresh parsley, chopped
- 1/4 cup fresh cilantro, chopped
- 1 tablespoon ground cumin
- 1 tablespoon ground coriander
- 1 teaspoon ground pepper
- 1 teaspoon baking powder
- Salt to taste
- 4-6 tablespoons flour
- Oil for frying

Instructions:

1. In a food processor, blend soaked chickpeas, onion, garlic, parsley, cilantro, cumin, coriander, pepper, and salt until coarse but well mixed.
2. Add baking powder and flour and blend until smooth enough to form a dough. Let it rest for 30 minutes.
3. Shape the dough into small balls or patties.
4. Heat oil in a pan or fryer to 375°F (190°C) and fry falafel until golden brown, about 3-4 minutes.
5. Serve with pita bread, hummus, or tahini sauce.

French Bouillabaisse

Ingredients:

- 1 lb firm white fish (such as cod or haddock), cut into pieces
- 1/2 lb shellfish (mussels, shrimp, or lobster)
- 1 onion, chopped
- 2 leeks, chopped
- 4 tomatoes, chopped
- 4 cloves garlic, minced
- 1/4 cup olive oil
- 1 teaspoon saffron threads
- 2 bay leaves
- 1 teaspoon thyme
- 1/2 teaspoon fennel seeds
- 4 cups fish stock
- 1/2 cup white wine
- Salt and pepper to taste
- Fresh parsley for garnish
- Crusty bread for serving

Instructions:

1. In a large pot, heat olive oil and sauté onions, leeks, and garlic until softened.
2. Add tomatoes, saffron, bay leaves, thyme, fennel, and fish stock. Bring to a boil, then simmer for 20 minutes.
3. Add the white fish and shellfish. Cook for another 10-15 minutes, until the fish is cooked through.
4. Stir in the white wine, and season with salt and pepper.
5. Serve the bouillabaisse with crusty bread and garnish with parsley.

Singapore Chili Crab

Ingredients:

- 2 crabs, cleaned and cut into pieces
- 1/4 cup vegetable oil
- 4 cloves garlic, minced
- 1-inch piece ginger, minced
- 2 red chilies, chopped
- 2 tablespoons tomato ketchup
- 2 tablespoons chili paste
- 1 tablespoon soy sauce
- 1 tablespoon sugar
- 1/2 cup water
- 1 egg, lightly beaten
- Salt and pepper to taste
- Fresh cilantro for garnish
- Steamed buns for serving

Instructions:

1. Heat oil in a large wok or skillet. Sauté garlic, ginger, and red chilies until fragrant.
2. Add tomato ketchup, chili paste, soy sauce, sugar, and water. Bring to a simmer.
3. Add crab pieces and cook for 8-10 minutes, stirring frequently.
4. Slowly add the beaten egg to thicken the sauce, stirring gently.
5. Season with salt and pepper, garnish with cilantro, and serve with steamed buns.

Thai Mango Sticky Rice

Ingredients:

- 1 cup sticky rice
- 1 1/2 cups coconut milk
- 1/2 cup sugar
- 1/4 teaspoon salt
- 2 ripe mangoes, peeled and sliced
- Sesame seeds or mung beans for garnish (optional)

Instructions:

1. Rinse sticky rice under cold water until the water runs clear. Steam the rice for 25-30 minutes, until soft.
2. In a saucepan, heat coconut milk, sugar, and salt until the sugar dissolves. Pour over the steamed rice and mix well.
3. Let the rice sit for 10-15 minutes to absorb the coconut milk.
4. Serve the sticky rice with sliced mango and garnish with sesame seeds or mung beans.

Chinese Kung Pao Chicken

Ingredients:

- 1 lb chicken breast, cut into small cubes
- 2 tablespoons soy sauce
- 2 teaspoons rice vinegar
- 1 teaspoon cornstarch
- 1 tablespoon vegetable oil
- 1/2 cup unsalted dry roasted peanuts
- 3-4 dried red chilies
- 4 cloves garlic, minced
- 1-inch piece ginger, minced
- 1/4 cup soy sauce
- 2 tablespoons hoisin sauce
- 1 tablespoon sugar
- 1/4 cup water
- 2 teaspoons cornstarch (for sauce)

Instructions:

1. In a bowl, mix chicken with 2 tablespoons soy sauce, rice vinegar, and 1 teaspoon cornstarch. Marinate for 15-20 minutes.
2. Heat vegetable oil in a wok over medium-high heat. Add the chicken and cook until browned and cooked through. Remove and set aside.
3. In the same wok, add dried chilies, garlic, and ginger, stir-frying for 1 minute.
4. Add soy sauce, hoisin sauce, sugar, water, and cornstarch. Bring to a simmer.
5. Return chicken to the wok, stir in peanuts, and cook for another 2-3 minutes until the sauce thickens.
6. Serve with steamed rice.

Indian Samosas

Ingredients:

- 2 cups boiled potatoes, mashed
- 1 cup cooked peas
- 1 tablespoon vegetable oil
- 1 onion, chopped
- 1 teaspoon cumin seeds
- 1 teaspoon coriander powder
- 1/2 teaspoon turmeric powder
- 1 teaspoon garam masala
- 2 tablespoons fresh cilantro, chopped
- Salt to taste
- 10-12 samosa wrappers (store-bought or homemade)
- Oil for frying

Instructions:

1. Heat oil in a pan and sauté onions until soft. Add cumin seeds, coriander powder, turmeric, and garam masala, and cook for 1 minute.
2. Add mashed potatoes, peas, cilantro, and salt. Mix well and cook for 5 minutes. Let the filling cool.
3. Fold samosa wrappers into cones, fill with the potato mixture, and seal the edges with water.
4. Heat oil in a pan and deep fry samosas until golden brown.
5. Serve with chutney or yogurt.

Italian Lasagna

Ingredients:

- 1 lb ground beef
- 1 onion, chopped
- 2 cloves garlic, minced
- 2 cups tomato sauce
- 1 teaspoon oregano
- 1 teaspoon basil
- 1/2 teaspoon salt
- 9 lasagna noodles, cooked and drained
- 2 cups ricotta cheese
- 2 cups mozzarella cheese, shredded
- 1/2 cup Parmesan cheese, grated

Instructions:

1. Preheat the oven to 375°F (190°C).
2. In a skillet, brown ground beef with onions and garlic. Add tomato sauce, oregano, basil, and salt. Simmer for 20 minutes.
3. In a separate bowl, combine ricotta, half the mozzarella, and Parmesan cheese.
4. In a baking dish, layer lasagna noodles, meat sauce, and cheese mixture. Repeat the layers and finish with cheese on top.
5. Bake for 30-40 minutes, until bubbly and golden. Let cool for 10 minutes before serving.

Moroccan Couscous

Ingredients:

- 2 cups couscous
- 2 cups vegetable broth
- 1 tablespoon olive oil
- 1/2 teaspoon cinnamon
- 1/2 teaspoon cumin
- 1/2 teaspoon turmeric
- Salt to taste
- 1/4 cup raisins
- 1/4 cup chopped almonds
- Fresh cilantro for garnish

Instructions:

1. Bring vegetable broth to a boil. Stir in couscous, olive oil, cinnamon, cumin, turmeric, and salt.
2. Cover and remove from heat. Let it steam for 5 minutes.
3. Fluff the couscous with a fork, then stir in raisins, almonds, and cilantro.
4. Serve as a side dish with tagine or grilled meats.

Filipino Lechon

Ingredients:

- 1 whole pig (or pork shoulder)
- 1/4 cup soy sauce
- 1/4 cup vinegar
- 1 tablespoon brown sugar
- 2 cloves garlic, minced
- 2 onions, quartered
- 1 bunch lemongrass, crushed
- Salt and pepper to taste

Instructions:

1. In a large bowl, combine soy sauce, vinegar, sugar, garlic, salt, and pepper. Marinate the pig for at least 12 hours, or overnight.
2. Stuff the pig with onions and lemongrass, and secure it on a roasting spit.
3. Roast over an open flame or in a large oven for 4-5 hours, until the skin is crispy and the meat is tender.
4. Serve with vinegar dipping sauce.

Persian Fesenjan

Ingredients:

- 2 chicken breasts or thighs, cut into pieces
- 1 onion, chopped
- 2 tablespoons vegetable oil
- 2 cups pomegranate juice
- 1/2 cup ground walnuts
- 1/2 teaspoon cinnamon
- 1/2 teaspoon turmeric
- 1/2 teaspoon cumin
- Salt and pepper to taste
- Fresh parsley for garnish
- Steamed rice for serving

Instructions:

1. In a pot, sauté onion in oil until golden brown. Add chicken pieces and cook until browned on all sides.
2. Stir in pomegranate juice, ground walnuts, cinnamon, turmeric, cumin, salt, and pepper. Bring to a boil.
3. Reduce heat and simmer for 45-60 minutes, until the sauce thickens and the chicken is tender.
4. Serve with steamed rice and garnish with fresh parsley.

German Sauerkraut with Sausages

Ingredients:

- 1 jar (about 24 oz) sauerkraut, drained
- 4 German sausages (bratwurst or other)
- 1 onion, sliced
- 2 cloves garlic, minced
- 1/2 cup white wine or beer
- 1 tablespoon olive oil
- 1 teaspoon caraway seeds
- 1 bay leaf
- Salt and pepper to taste
- Fresh parsley for garnish

Instructions:

1. Heat olive oil in a large skillet or pot. Add onions and garlic and sauté until softened.
2. Add sauerkraut, wine or beer, caraway seeds, and bay leaf. Stir to combine and bring to a simmer.
3. Season with salt and pepper, then cover and simmer on low for about 30 minutes.
4. Grill or pan-fry the sausages until browned and cooked through.
5. Serve sausages over the sauerkraut, garnished with fresh parsley.

Greek Souvlaki

Ingredients:

- 1 lb boneless chicken, pork, or lamb, cut into cubes
- 3 tablespoons olive oil
- 2 tablespoons lemon juice
- 2 cloves garlic, minced
- 1 teaspoon dried oregano
- 1/2 teaspoon ground cumin
- Salt and pepper to taste
- 1 pita bread or flatbreads
- Fresh vegetables for serving (tomatoes, cucumbers, onions)
- Tzatziki sauce

Instructions:

1. In a bowl, combine olive oil, lemon juice, garlic, oregano, cumin, salt, and pepper. Marinate the meat for at least 1 hour or overnight.
2. Thread the marinated meat onto skewers and grill or cook on a skillet over medium-high heat for 8-10 minutes, turning occasionally, until cooked through.
3. Warm the pita bread on the grill.
4. Serve the souvlaki on pita with fresh vegetables and a generous amount of tzatziki sauce.

Caribbean Callaloo Soup

Ingredients:

- 1 bunch callaloo (or substitute with spinach)
- 1 tablespoon vegetable oil
- 1 onion, chopped
- 2 cloves garlic, minced
- 1 bell pepper, chopped
- 1 tomato, chopped
- 4 cups chicken broth
- 1/2 cup coconut milk
- 1/2 teaspoon thyme
- 1/2 teaspoon allspice
- 1 Scotch bonnet pepper (optional, for heat)
- Salt and pepper to taste
- 1/2 cup cooked crab meat or smoked fish (optional)
- Fresh lime for garnish

Instructions:

1. Heat vegetable oil in a large pot. Add onions, garlic, and bell pepper, and sauté until softened.
2. Add tomatoes, chicken broth, coconut milk, thyme, allspice, and Scotch bonnet pepper (if using). Bring to a boil and simmer for 15 minutes.
3. Add the callaloo (or spinach) and cook for an additional 5-7 minutes until the greens are tender.
4. Stir in crab meat or smoked fish (if desired), season with salt and pepper.
5. Serve the soup with a squeeze of fresh lime.

Malaysian Laksa

Ingredients:

- 200g rice noodles
- 1 tablespoon vegetable oil
- 200g chicken breast or shrimp, cooked and shredded or peeled
- 1/2 cup coconut milk
- 2 cups chicken broth
- 1 tablespoon red curry paste
- 1 tablespoon tamarind paste
- 1 tablespoon fish sauce
- 1 teaspoon sugar
- 2 boiled eggs, halved
- Fresh cilantro and bean sprouts for garnish

Instructions:

1. Cook rice noodles according to package instructions. Set aside.
2. In a pot, heat vegetable oil and sauté curry paste until fragrant.
3. Add chicken broth, coconut milk, tamarind paste, fish sauce, and sugar. Bring to a simmer and cook for 10 minutes.
4. Add cooked chicken or shrimp into the soup and heat through.
5. To serve, place noodles in a bowl, pour the soup over, and top with boiled eggs, fresh cilantro, and bean sprouts.

Egyptian Molokhia

Ingredients:

- 2 cups molokhia leaves (or substitute with spinach)
- 4 cups chicken broth
- 4 cloves garlic, minced
- 2 tablespoons ghee or vegetable oil
- 1 teaspoon ground coriander
- 1 teaspoon cumin
- 1 tablespoon lemon juice
- Salt and pepper to taste
- 1 lb chicken, cooked and shredded (optional)
- Rice for serving

Instructions:

1. In a pot, heat ghee or oil and sauté garlic until fragrant. Add ground coriander and cumin and cook for another minute.
2. Pour in the chicken broth, bring to a boil, and then add molokhia leaves. Simmer for 10-15 minutes until the leaves are tender.
3. Add lemon juice and season with salt and pepper.
4. Serve the molokhia over rice with the shredded chicken (optional).

Italian Osso Buco

Ingredients:

- 4 veal shanks (or beef shanks)
- 1/4 cup flour
- 2 tablespoons olive oil
- 1 onion, chopped
- 2 carrots, chopped
- 2 celery stalks, chopped
- 4 cloves garlic, minced
- 1 cup dry white wine
- 2 cups beef broth
- 1 can (14.5 oz) crushed tomatoes
- 1 teaspoon dried thyme
- 1 bay leaf
- Salt and pepper to taste
- Gremolata (chopped parsley, garlic, lemon zest) for garnish

Instructions:

1. Dredge veal shanks in flour. Heat olive oil in a large pot over medium-high heat. Brown the shanks on all sides, then remove them.
2. In the same pot, sauté onions, carrots, celery, and garlic until softened.
3. Add white wine to deglaze the pot, scraping up any browned bits. Add beef broth, crushed tomatoes, thyme, bay leaf, salt, and pepper.
4. Return the veal shanks to the pot and cover. Simmer on low heat for 2-3 hours until the meat is tender.
5. Serve with gremolata on top.

Turkish Kebab

Ingredients:

- 1 lb ground lamb or beef
- 1 onion, finely chopped
- 2 cloves garlic, minced
- 1 teaspoon cumin
- 1 teaspoon paprika
- 1/2 teaspoon ground coriander
- Salt and pepper to taste
- Fresh parsley, chopped
- Pita or flatbread for serving

Instructions:

1. In a bowl, combine ground meat, onion, garlic, cumin, paprika, coriander, salt, and pepper. Mix well.
2. Shape the mixture into long, sausage-like kebabs and thread onto skewers.
3. Grill the kebabs on medium-high heat for 5-7 minutes, turning occasionally until cooked through.
4. Serve the kebabs in pita or flatbread with fresh parsley and your favorite dipping sauce.

Jamaican Patties

Ingredients:

- 1 lb ground beef or chicken
- 1 tablespoon vegetable oil
- 1 onion, chopped
- 1 clove garlic, minced
- 1 tablespoon curry powder
- 1/2 teaspoon thyme
- 1/2 teaspoon allspice
- 1/4 teaspoon Scotch bonnet pepper (optional)
- 1/4 cup breadcrumbs
- 1/4 cup beef or chicken broth
- 1 pack of store-bought or homemade pastry dough

Instructions:

1. Heat oil in a pan and sauté onions and garlic until soft.
2. Add ground meat and cook until browned, breaking it up into small pieces.
3. Stir in curry powder, thyme, allspice, and Scotch bonnet pepper. Add breadcrumbs and broth, and simmer until the filling thickens.
4. Roll out the pastry dough and cut into circles. Place the filling in the center of each circle, fold the dough over, and crimp the edges to seal.
5. Bake at 375°F (190°C) for 20-25 minutes, until golden brown.

Venezuelan Arepas

Ingredients:

- 2 cups pre-cooked cornmeal (masarepa)
- 2 cups warm water
- 1 tablespoon vegetable oil
- 1 teaspoon salt
- Fillings (cheese, shredded beef, chicken, avocado)

Instructions:

1. In a bowl, combine masarepa, warm water, oil, and salt. Mix until dough forms. Let it rest for 5 minutes.
2. Shape the dough into small patties.
3. Heat a skillet over medium heat and cook the arepas for 4-5 minutes on each side, until golden brown.
4. Slice open the arepas and stuff with your desired fillings, such as cheese, shredded beef, or chicken.